The Leader You Choose to Be

Straightforward Leadership Strategies I Learned by Working in Silicon Valley

OVIDILIO DAVID VASQUEZ

Foreword by

Dr. Nicholas Valenzuela, Ph.D.

FOREWORD

Ovidilio Vasquez has written an abridged and insightful book about leadership based on his incredible journey from a farmboy working in sugarcane fields in rural Guatemala to a white-collar professional working at some of the world's most prestigious companies in Silicon Valley, such as Salesforce, Tesla, Apple, and others. His story is inspiring to everyone who reads this book. He is a TEDx Speaker, has written several national best-selling books, and is a highly sought-after motivational speaker on leadership.

In my career as a college professor, a business leader in Silicon Valley, and a coach who strives to instill a sense of self-confidence and agency in my clients and mentees, I have never met anyone as inspiring and motivating as Ovi. As an adviser and consultant to top Silicon executives at companies such as Microsoft, Sun Microsystems, Seagate Technologies, and other Fortune 100 companies, I know how critical leadership is to corporate and personal success. For example, at Seagate Technologies, while working as a strategic planning manager, the data and analysis I shared with the company's top executives and leadership led them to make decisions that grew the company from under $1 billion in annual revenue to nearly $4 billion in a few short years and to become a $12+ billion corporation.

When I met Ovidilio David Vasquez, I knew he was a unique individual destined for greatness, destined to lead and inspire others. He is courageous, daring, confident, and inspiring. He is an optimist, inspired by the many opportunities that life offers and not dissuaded by obstacles others find insurmountable. People are inspired by his passion and the success he has achieved. He shows us that life's challenges can be overcome with confidence and assurance and encourages us to recognize the greatness in all of us to be leaders and be successful.

Ovidilio Vasquez has inspired countless, from realtors and sales professionals to rank-and-file employees and students at colleges and universities, to become leaders and successful with their work, careers, and personal lives. His message is clear that we all have inside of us what it takes to succeed, that there is a leader in all of us, and that our actions, more than our words, make us leaders and successful. He urges us to lead by example, models leadership by his behavior, and takes responsibility for his success as a means of inspiring us to do the same.

This book will inspire you to become an influential leader, approach life with optimism, and have confidence that you will be successful. You will be inspired by the leadership principles he describes, by his passion and optimism for life, and by his story of immigrating to the United States and transforming himself into a leader and successful keynote motivational speaker. I urge everyone to read it.

Nicholas A. Valenzuela, Ph.D., Stanford University
Inspiring people to achieve greatness in their lives.

CONTENTS

This page was intentionally left blank

INTRODUCTION

In 2012 I was part of a large multi-level marketing business. One of the required books to read was a book called, *"Skills With People."* The main reason I am mentioning this book at the very beginning of my book—is that that book was required reading for tens of thousands of distributors. The book was less than 25 pages long. The book was compelling and insightful. It was an easy read, and it was engaging. Every sentence contained lots of value. Anyone could pick up the book and be almost certain that they could have finished this book within an hour, no matter how slow they read. In this abridge written version of the insights I share, my goal is for your to gain these insights in less than an hour. True leaders recognize valuable information and share it to develop more leaders.

I have never been a big reader. Imagine being born and growing up on a tiny farm in the sugarcane fields of Central America. No electricity. Every day, I would be outdoors raising chickens, pigs, and animals on the farm owned by my grandmother. After sixth grade, I did not go to the seventh grade, and I went straight to work in the fields, harvesting mango, plating and cutting sugarcane, harvesting bananas, and working in several labor-heavy jobs under the hot, humid weather. No one in my family or community emphasized the importance of reading any books, maybe because there are no libraries around in a 20 miles radius. The book mentioned earlier seemed easy to read because of its size, so I read it several times.

The book you have in your hands now is not good—unless you go through it entirely, maybe even more than once. I made it short and to the point. I will share only the things that matter. Maybe one line or more will make it worth the investment in time into developing yourself personally and professionally through this book. Throughout, you will find ideas that will sparkle in your mind that could change your day, week, month, quarter, or an entire year in your career. You are about to learn the ideas and information; I discovered while working for some of the most globally recognized brands, such as Apple, Tesla, Salesforce, Uber, and a startup acquired by General Motors.

The organizations I mentioned have designed, distributed, and sold revolutionary technologies that have impacted millions of lives. Whether you think the effect is positive or negative—that is up to your perspective, but we cannot ignore the fact that they have experienced massive growth at a rapid pace. Therefore, everything you will learn here is designed to help you generate ideas and strategies to implement in your day-to-day professional life— maybe even in your personal life. You can create a future where you will see rapid growth and increase your chances for success, no matter what success.

This page was intentionally left blank

BELIEF

Believe you can achieve more. The more you can believe you can achieve, the more your team will accomplish. Therefore, your confidence should radiate and transmit a high level of competency.

Working with a team requires strategic thinking and in-depth vision. Strategic thinking will get you to radiate the confidence you need to transmit to your team members to feel that they can execute on what you have planned for your quarterly or yearly goals. Unless you genuinely believe you can achieve the strategy you have in mind, which you also should have on paper—these days—even on digital form, it will be difficult for your team members to follow your leadership instinctively.

You may have heard a variation of the following phrase; *"Some people light up a room when they walk into it,*

1

and some light it up when they walk out of it." People often use the phrase when referring to a person's attitude. When I worked at Salesforce, a hyper-growth multi-billion-dollar technology company, the internal operations thrived because of the feeling the leaders transmitted to their teams. When you share your confidence and belief that you can achieve the strategy you are presenting to your team, you create a high probability of success. You will see your plan come to fruition. Design your *"game plan"* with everyone's talents in mind. Then, communicate the vision of what it will feel to attain success. Do keep this in mind; Be willing to fail while working on achieving the results planned.

Your team members might sometimes question your level of competency. Some of them might believe they are more qualified than you to execute the ideas you have put forth. Some of them could feel they deserve your role as a leader. They express these inconformities non-verbally with how they react to what you say and how they act with the plans, ideas, and requests you make for the team. But you know your title as a leader was not *"given"* to you. You earned it. As their leader, knowing this, now you see why it is paramount that you always radiate a high level of confidence and competence. Do the doing because, as you know, leadership is not only about talking; it is mainly about walking the talk.

Can your team believe they can achieve the goals you set for them?

The concepts, ideas, and strategies you will read in this book are not new, and you have probably already heard of them before. Precisely like your team, oftentimes—when you share with them a strategy, they may think you are not sharing anything new. However, that is far from the truth. The difference is; An idea shared with the same person when the person is in a different state of mind; the concept will sound completely different than when first presented to them. Likewise, this book may trigger new ideas for solutions to problems you might have dealt with—for a long time. Share with your team why you believe your strategy will work.

If your team feels they heard your idea before, they may or might not want to execute it. Be mentally and emotionally prepared to overcome these obstacles. The pushback can be temporary. The answer to many questions you may be thinking about; find them here. Leverage your in-depth vision. Be a conscious competent leader. Here, you will find the tools, strategies, and ideas to overcome these obstacles. Identify oppositions that frequently come as pushback from your team by paying keen attention to the following: Their choice of words. The behavior they display. The attitude they put forth at different times of the day may bring your entire team's morale down.

When you see this idea as I am sharing with you and you think to yourself, *"I already know this. I already heard this,"* allow me to share the three most dangerous words that I have learned in the English language. There are only three of them. And these are the three most dangerous words I have learned. ***"I know that."*** Yes, as soon a leader thinks they know what is being presented to them, in that very second, it closes their mind. A closed mind misses learning opportunities.

I am sharing what could be a refresher to remember a lesson you have learned.
Does it bring up an existing strategy you know? Has it reinforced an idea you have heard before? Now could be the right time to implement this idea with your team. You can directly transmit the belief that you can achieve a target result with your strategy. Because when you designed this strategy, you created it with their gifts, talents, and skills in mind. Now you know your team members can execute this strategy. It is up to you to start.
How will you present these strategies to them? What level of energy, gusto, and enthusiasm will you display when you decide to share these ideas with them? Their level of belief will depend on that. They will pick up from you to achieve these by working together with you.

In the next chapter, you will learn to build that

image that tells everyone around you, in your home, in your home office, who you are and what you are all about so that they can be influenced by your image, your brand—even before you speak a single word.

BRAND IMPACT

Building your impactful brand may be a new concept to many people. The primary sector that I have heard of is the technology sector. After traveling nationwide to different companies and organizations, I don't listen to it being a conversation topic. People like to follow someone they can aspire to model. Design your public profiles, and showcase your mission and the work you are continuously doing. When your customers and everyone you want to engage with see it—they will know they are following a doer, not a talker. They are supporting a leader. Support, as you know, can be in the following form:

Bringing more business to you.

Working extra hours for you.

Helping you broaden your brand's reach.

Interacting with you online to help trigger the algorithm.

Learning a new skill to help execute your proposed ideas.

Talented individuals want to follow the advice and the directions of someone they respect. Build your impactful brand, personally and professionally. They will aspire to make you proud of the results they will produce by the requests you make of them. Your team members respect a certain level of respect. Some only require minimal things to know so they can follow your instruction. However, high-standard individuals have higher expectations as to their behavior. Unless your values and principles are congruent with your behavior, they will not follow, at least now happily.

What is the reason they should even listen to you?

What are you requesting them to do?

If they agree to your requests, they perform out of obligation, not respect. Control your personal power, values, morals, and principles. Control your behavior. By controlling your physiology, you will influence your attitude. They will respect that of you.

People check their co-workers' social media— sometimes, they even do it while on the clock. If you think they do not look for you, well, they probably do. People's social media profiles and what they share online are available to nearly anyone with an internet connection. People get rejected for job opportunities, and deals get canceled. Conclusions are made based on what people share. Even though it is their personal opinion, it is on their time, likes, and desires. People will judge you by that—when you publicly share this content on various platforms online. The content they disagree with. If you think this cannot affect you, it would be a great idea to consider thinking again.

You may say, *"I have my personal beliefs, and I'm going to stick to them no matter what."* I am only here to remind you that these could lead to your team members seeing what you share. They will create their own ideas and decide whether they want to listen to you or they will begin to find their **"exit strategy"** from your organization. Culture is of utmost importance for talented professionals. As you may have heard, in sales, *"People like to buy from people they Know, Like, and Trust."* It works the same with the talented individuals you lead. They need to; Know you. Like you. Trust you.

You may think to yourself, *"Wait a minute, they are part of my team. They get paid to do the work; that is what they get paid to do, so why would not they do the work?"* Because people are more deeply motivated by the company's mission than by what they get paid in every paycheck. Doing the work that they do is meaningful to them. It is an art. If they see your incongruencies on or off the internet, they will not be open to your leadership. They notice details in every conversation in your daily behavior. I am not saying you are doing something inappropriate; I do not know you. I do not know your belief system. I am making you aware that they will decide by building their subjective personal opinion on your behavior.

If what you share outside of work contradicts what

your company is all about, there is a conflict. Your values and behavior should align as close as possible if you expect your team to do things in a certain way. Your guidelines expect them to behave in a certain way. Your protocol says to deal with customers in a specific manner. Then, they see in your profiles that you argue with people about the color of a vehicle, a particular object, or a particular organization. They will know that you are an argumentative individual. Being confrontational is not a quality of a leader. Yet at work, you expect them to do any different when they deal with their colleagues or their customers, their clients. It is almost like the phrase, **"Do as I say, not as I do."** Talented professionals do not respect that. People tend to think, *"But, if I am off., I am off."* referring to lowering their behavior standards when not at work. A wise phrase says, *"How you do anything is how you do everything."* And I would like to add a personal favorite, *"Integrity is what you do when no one is looking."*

Build your brand, make it impactful. Show that you are congruent with your words, values, and behavior at work and off work. They will respect that about you—especially if they agree with what you showcase. When they see it, they know they are following a role model of great character. Even if you do not have an **"official"** title of a leader role at work, you are still a leader worth following because you are a respectable individual in their eyes.

The opinions you may have, the behavior you may portray, may not be something that I agree with, but I do not matter in this equation. What matters is you, your team, and your company's mission. When everything is aligned, they know that it's not about the compensation. Possibly they are not going to get paid overtime. Often they do not get paid extra benefits or get paid additional vacations. Your talented team will want to support you with your mission and strategy. Because of the leader, you are because you have earned their respect.

In some organizations, when a leader leaves, no matter the reason, that leader's team often quits and follows their leader to the next organization. *Why is that?* Because of the impactful brand they built, that built respect and loyalty in your team members will have influence and impact. Make sure it is a positive impact.

In the next chapter, you are going to learn how to become a mentor to planters, which will multiply and lead you to see results beyond what many people expect from you. See you in the next chapter.

MENTORSHIP

Become a mentor to a planter. A planter is a leader who will use what you give them and multiply it to benefit others. Identify a planter to mentor, not necessarily younger than you, and always remember you are a leader. With this in mind, you trust that you have something valuable to share. Whether product knowledge, strategy, motivation, or personal advice, you have something valuable to share. Your expertise does no good—unless you share it with your team. If you share it with someone who keeps the knowledge to themselves, the wisdom, the strategy, the idea, and they do nothing with it, your idea will die. It will not make any further impact. There will be no ripple effect—you might have wasted your valuable time.

When you identify a person who enjoys developing their team—even cross teams in different departments. You know you may be sharing this knowledge with the right person because they will take the impact even further. Even when you are sleeping, they may be impacting others to help them grow. Imagine this for a moment; You experience a ***"Eureka moment"*** in which you think of an idea that can positively impact the numbers for the next quarter when implemented. You go and share it with the most enthusiastic connector in your team because you know that they will share this idea with everyone else, and it will spread like wildfire. When it spreads, what will happen is that there will be a level of enthusiasm built, which should increase the morale in your team.

When you increase the morale in your team by what you did or by what you are doing, or by what you will be doing, they will be more energetic to execute their day-to-day tasks. And, because they will be more vibrant and calm, no chaos will overtake them. Your team will become more creative in implementing ideas, and their innovative power will help them perform with a sense of urgency. Fast doesn't always mean best, but speed is necessary for execution so you can find results quickly. One of the primary ways to get ahead of the competition is to find results quickly so you can make immediately carefully-calculated adjustments. You can adjust the strategy when you see the result is not the result you were expecting. Talented individuals tend to be creative during certain times throughout the day, and it is different for everyone. Identify when and where they perform at their best, then pair them. Highly-competent creative team members executing at their peak performance, collaborating will almost guarantee you that your team will always win.

You decide to swap who should work on the strategy and at what point they should join. Get to know your team—you can schedule weekly or bi-weekly one-to-one 15 minutes meetings—even better, enjoy lunch with them. Find out what motivates them to perform at their best. Based on what you know about your team:

What are the best tools to you use?

When is the best time to work on your plan?

Are you providing the training and tools to your team?

What is the most optimal timeline to make these plans come to fruition?

Be reasonable to achieve a higher quality of success when you get the result of these projects to accomplish your qualitative or quantitative targets.

How did it all start? By planting a seed in one person who then went out and shared it with everybody else. Be careful because if you plant the wrong seed—the wrong idea will go out to the team, and you could lose everybody because the connector will connect with them. That is their nature. Make sure the seed is always a positive one. You, as the leader, are the strategic thinker. You have ideation power. You have the position and have the ***"official"*** title. Most importantly, you make the decision you share with them.

You cannot always control how they execute—even though you expect them to perform in a certain way at a certain speed. We cannot control our team members' performance because we cannot control their daily lives. Their everyday life affects their state of being, affecting their energy level, affecting their performance. The affairs in their personal everyday life are often constantly changing. They could be experiencing conflict with their spouse or having issues with their kids—their pet could be sick. People and things they are emotionally attached to could affect them. When you know how to identify this—you know you are a leader who understands Emotional Intelligence.

As leaders, we cannot blame ourselves for the missed targets. Do not take things too personally when the outcome is not what you expected. It's about taking responsibility, not blame. True leaders have no time for blame. Leaders carefully study the result, then swiftly develop an alternative strategy based on what I shared earlier. You can plant the seed of greatness of this great idea of this strategy that you know will work. Share that with someone that will take it even farther than you can. Create a ripple effect, a positive effect.

Growing up, when we used to plant corn, we would plant three single corns in the ground, faithfully work daily to take care of the corn, carefully care for the corn plant, and in return, it would give us beautiful corn in abundance. Imagine you go to work on Tuesday, and you only work four hours because you have a short shift. You go home, do something else, and the person you shared that idea with stays within the company to work a full day of work. They will take your impact even farther—even when you are not present.

What is your team member going to say on your behalf?
How will this person present your strategy on your behalf?
How is that person going to communicate your idea on your behalf?

It depends on how you transmitted it to them. It depends on how you shared it with them. It depends on how you present it to them. It depends on what energy level you transmitted to them while sharing it with them. Be aware of your competency. Be mindful of your energy level. Be aware of your attitude. Be cognizant of your behavior in and out of the office because the most important person will always be watching—that person is the one you see in the mirror.

Be careful in becoming a leader who sabotages themselves, especially when we know we are not doing what we preach. We know that we could be doing better, and we have the potential to become better. We know our team works with us, not for us. Your team will feel you as the person that you are. It is not about being a coworker, manager, supervisor, or regional manager. It is not about the business. It is always about the people. Your team will uplift you as high as you inspire them.

You have control over yourself. If you keep control over yourself, as a competent leader, you will know what to say when you speak to each team member, and how you say it to them is not always how they will understand it. Have you heard of the golden rule; *"Treat others the way you would like to be treated?"* With talented professionals, the platinum rule may serve you best; *"Treat others the way they want to be treated."*

Frequently, words are mistaken in perspective because you said a phrase, and they misunderstood it. As a leader, it is imperative always to be proactive. Before our team members proceed and make a mistake and share the wrong idea with everyone else, have the dialogue and say, *"Could you please share with me, in your own words, what is the message you will share with the rest of our team?"* When your team member shares with you how he understood what you said, now you verified that he understood what you meant. Now you know you have planted the good seed, and now you can expect not only a good harvest but a great harvest because you have planted a good seed on a planter— pat yourself on the back. You deserve recognition.

CONCLUSION

I made a promise to you. I was going to make this book short. Hopefully, you read it within an hour. Some of you probably read it within ten minutes. I am glad that you have come across this book, these ideas, and these strategies. As simple as it may be, these are powerful because I acquired these ideas and strategies by working for the corporations I mentioned in the introduction.

The reason why I wrote this book is that I believe you are a planter. Plant on fertile ground. Sometimes the soil is not fertile, and you may have to prepare before it can take seeds. The same concept works with people. You will have to train them to the competence level you need them to be. A true leader makes an impact beyond his lifetime. The organization you are part of has a mission, and this mission is greater than the profits generated by the sales made every year.

Now, you can take this knowledge and these ideas and do what you will with them. You have the power to make a positive impact on someone's life. Please share this with your friends; maybe some of them are entrepreneurial, and by implementing these ideas in their small businesses could become large enterprises. Of course, there is so much more to be shared. Even though I have shared a good seed with you, the seed will need lots of care, lots of watering, lots of good intention, so it becomes fruitful at the right time.

We will be putting together tailored workshops where you will be able to access via your mobile devices to learn more in an easy-to-learn format. Our goal is to help you transmit this energy to everyone on your team, and in return, they will reciprocate. When you go home at the end of the day, and someone you care about asks, *"How did your day go?"* You can genuinely say, *"It went great!"*

When you take it day-by-day, you create an excellent week, and you can duplicate the process until you make a year of excellence. It is an honor to be of service to you. I shared these insights with you—with great intention. Thank you already for the impact you make.

ABOUT THE AUTHOR

Ovidilio David Vasquez is a National Leadership Keynote Speaker, a TEDx Speaker, and the author of six books, including a #1 Bestseller. He went from being a farmboy raised in a tiny ranch near a poor village in the sugarcane fields of Central America to working for global companies like; Apple, Tesla, Salesforce, Uber, and General Motors.

In 2019, he was accepted to Harvard Business School Online. He is now working on a Specialization in Leadership and Management. Ovi believes in constant growth to better serve others. He has helped thousands nationwide by sharing over $1.5 million in available scholarships for college students through social media.

Large organizations benefit from his leadership insights, which he acquired by working at the companies mentioned earlier.

His favorite hobby is to dance Latin music with his two babies, Emy and David.

For more information about Ovidilio, go to:
OVinspires.com

For more information about this book, go to:
TheLeaderYouChooseToBe.com
This page was intentionally left blank

This page was intentionally left blank

46458477R00018